animal babies

in towns and cities

KINGFISHER

Kingfisher Publications Plc
New Penderel House
283–288 High Holborn
London WC1V 7HZ
www.kingfisherpub.com

First published by Kingfisher Publications Plc 2005
10 9 8 7 6 5 4 3 2 1
1TR/0505/TWP/SGCH(SGCH)/150STORA/C
Copyright © Kingfisher Publications Plc 2005

A CIP catalogue record for this book is available from the British Library.

ISBN–13: 978 0 7534 1108 7
ISBN–10: 0 7534 1108 3

Author and Editor: Jennifer Schofield
Designer: Joanne Brown
Picture Manager: Cee Weston-Baker
Picture Researcher: Rachael Swann
DTP Co-ordinator: Carsten Lorenz
Production Controller: Jessamy Oldfield

Printed in Singapore

animal babies

in towns and cities

When I find **nuts** and acorns, I bury them in the soil. I dig them up when I am hungry.

Who is my mummy?

My **mummy** is a squirrel and I am her **kitten**.

We have **big**, bushy tails. We use them to **balance** along **narrow** branches.

During the day I like to rest. But, at night, I wander around the town looking for food.

Who is my mummy?

My mummy is a red fox and I am her cub.

When I am older, my brown coat will turn rusty red, just like my mummy's.

I have dark, black patches around my beady eyes. It looks like I am wearing a mask.

Who is my mummy?

My mummy
is a raccoon and
I am her cub.

We are very good at
smelling, so we know
which rubbish bins will
be filled with tasty treats.

When big animals make me scared, I keep still and pretend to be dead so that they leave me alone.

Who is my mummy?

My mummy is a Virginia opossum and I am her joey.

I stay in my mummy's pouch until I can climb up trees on my own.

When I am young, my feathers are grey and fluffy. But, when I am older, they will be brown and sleek.

Who is my mummy?

My mummy is a peregrine falcon and I am her chick.

Until I can fly as fast as my mummy, I will stay in our nest at the top of the building.

I have very sharp claws on my paws. I use them to dig in the garden for juicy insects to eat.

Who is my mummy?

My mummy
is a skunk and
I am her kit.

If you frighten us,
we will spray you
with a horrible,
smelly oil.

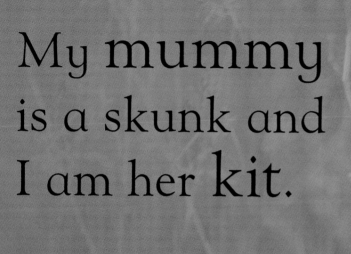

When I feel afraid,
I curl up into a ball
and make my sharp
spines stand on end.

Who is my mummy?

My mummy is
a hedgehog and
I am her hoglet.

During the winter,
we sleep in our nest.
But in summer, we
play in the garden.

Additional Information

Urban areas are home to many different animals, including marsupials such as Virginia opossums and mustelids such as skunks. As cities expand, the natural habitats of many animals are destroyed, and they are forced to adapt to living in urban areas: peregrine falcons use the ledges of high-rise buildings as inland cliffs on which to build their nests and raccoons use their dextrous paws to scavenge for food in rubbish bins. Animals such as hedgehogs, grey squirrels and red foxes rely on gardens for food and shelter.

Acknowledgements

The publisher would like to thank the following for permission to reproduce their material. Every care has been taken to trace copyright holders. However, if there have been unintentional omissions or failure to trace copyright holders, we apologise and will, if informed, endeavour to make corrections in any future edition.

Cover: Frank Lane Picture Agency (FLPA)/S+D+K Maslowski; Half title: Corbis/D Robert Franz; Title page: FLPA/ S+D+K Maslowski; Squirrel 1: Minden/Sumio Harada; Squirrel 2: Minden/Sumio Harada; Red fox 1: FLPA/ S+D+K Maslowski; Red fox 2: NHPA/Andy Rouse; Raccoon 1: Corbis/D Robert Franz; Raccoon 2: Oxford Scientific Films; Virginia opossum 1: FLPA/S+D+K Maslowski; Virginia opossum 2: FLPA/S+D+K Maslowski; Peregrine falcon 1: Corbis/Annie Griffiths Belt; Peregrine falcon 2: Corbis/Galen Rowell; Skunk 1: Corbis/ D Robert Franz; Skunk 2: Nature Picture Library/Jeff Foott; Hedgehog 1: Corbis/Maurizio Lanini; Hedgehog 2: NHPA/Manfred Danegger